AVOIDING THE RAPTURE

Karen J. Weyant

Riot in Your Throat
publishing fierce, feminist poetry

Weyant, Karen J.
1st edition.
ISBN: 978-1-73631386-9-4

Cover Art: Jody Glosser
Cover Design: Kirsten Birst
Book Design: Shanna Compton
Author Photo: Jodie Beabout

Riot in Your Throat
Arlington, VA
www.riotinyourthroat.com

For all the Rust Belt Girls who survived the Rapture. We made it.

CONTENTS

III.

TIPS FOR YOUNG GIRLS HOPING TO AVOID THE RAPTURE

Snag your new tights with rough edges of your fingernails.
Rip the seams on your spaghetti strapped sundresses.

Skip your baths. Don't brush. Floss your teeth with licorice lace candy.
Go to bed without combing the knots from your hair.

Wear grass stains on the knees of your jeans, splatter mud
all over your pink shirts. Step on every sidewalk crack.

Look one way when crossing the street. Steal communion wafers
and wine, drink until your lips and tongue turn scarlet.

Skip Sunday School lessons to skinny-dip in Tom Stetson's Pond.
Then, lie about where you've been, what you've been doing.

Practice swearing, use God's name in vain. Ignore
your parents. Take that one forbidden shortcut home:

the alley behind the bars on West Main. Watch the bartenders
step out the back door on break. Covet their tight jeans,

their t-shirts and tank tops, the cigarette smoke that drifts
from their mouths and fingers. On your way home, find

treasures: flattened pennies on rusted rails, daisies tangled
in weeds, a rhinestone earring that catches the streetlight,

lace panties and bras left hanging on clotheslines overnight.
When everyone disappears, everything you see will be yours.

I.

AUDITIONING FOR THE APOCALYPSE

Every girl I knew got religion
at the same time they caught Disco Fever.
Cheeks flushed, lips bright red,
they shivered in the stifling heat,
practiced the hustle in their bedrooms

and backyards. They ironed
their hair flat, wore flared jeans
and tube tops, thin elastic catching
sweat that pooled in their collar bones,
dripped down their shoulder blades.

We're waiting for the wapture,
lisped my best friend, as she showed me
her moves, all jerky shoulder rocks
and pelvic thrusts. We spilled out
onto the front sidewalk, skinny thighs

twitching to imaginary music.
Tarantella, muttered old Mrs. Fiorentino,
who dismissed our frenzied steps
with a wave of her broom. Brushing
dry leaves from her porch, swiping

a stray cobweb from the banisters,
she explained our dancing could cure
us all from a deadly spider's bite.
We knew we were already saved.
Throwing craft store glitter on our skin

we shimmered through seams
of our cutoff jeans. We bathed
in sidewalk steam after thunderstorms.
Facing uncertain futures,
we waited to be whisked away in sparkle.

CHAPSTICK

Little girls in small towns love
their ChapStick: vanilla bean,
Coca Cola, root beer. They dig
in their mothers' purses,
fingering loose pennies
and half sticks of bubble gum,
searching for the elusive lip balm.
They beg for extra money
in checkout lines, longing
for flavors that taunt them
from the shelves.
They know the smooth wax soothes
split lips parched in the dead-
dry months of winter.
They watch their mothers
rub lotion through the pinched
lines around their eyes, favorite
aunts smooth oil on their torn
cuticles. Even their older sisters
dot snags in their nylons
with clear fingernail polish.
They already believe there are salves
for all the raw wounds the women
around them are forced to wear:
rough elbows and heels, paper cuts,
deep gashes that never healed, but
turned to scabs, and then scars.

THE SPRING OF HAND-ME-DOWNS

That year my sister moved back home.
She's going through a bad spell,
said my mother. There was no talk about the ring
of white skin where a wedding band used to be.
For weeks, we tripped over her suitcases
left packed in the front hall and I waited

for the attention from the sister who taught me
that scrubbing my face with lemons would make
all of my freckles disappear. But there was nothing
except a shadow who sat on the back porch,
night after night, coffee cup in her hand,
and Marlboro packs crumpled at her feet.

Years before, I had inherited her platform shoes,
and two garbage bags full of clothes and because
the adult talk was about permanent layoffs,
I knew this spring there would be nothing new.
Modeling her bell-bottom jeans that dragged
on the floor, I hunched forward in a tube top,

and teetered to her evening vigil, waiting
for her advice about college or boys,
but she only frowned, smoke rings
surrounding us, *You know*, she said,
smashing her cigarette stub into
an ashtray made in a junior high shop class,
There is no way those pants go with that shirt.

THE (ALMOST) LOST LEGEND OF THE LAWSON BOYS

They spit tobacco juice in clear Mason jars
and smoked cigarette butts they found

smoldering on the cracked sidewalk.
They wore t-shirts with Budweiser logos

and old jeans stained with spaghetti sauce.
All learned to cuss early, the youngest

swearing through two missing front teeth
and a slight lisp. I watched them from

my Big Wheels perch, skinny legs stretched
in front of me, barely reaching the plastic pedals.

When they got too loud, my mother always
called me inside. She didn't want me to see

how they drank Pepsi for breakfast or ate
leftover pizza and black licorice for lunch.

She didn't want me to watch them playing
chicken on their bikes, riding head-on

into each other, yelling whenever one swerved
sideways into flying gravel and dust.

When they moved away, weeds cloaked
the front lawn overnight. The *For Sale* grew rusty.

For weeks, I looked for aluminum cans, ashes,
a bicycle spoke, anything that said they were once real.

TO THE GIRL WHO CAN HEAR THE RIVER TALK

You were born the year of a sudden spring melt,
of a heavy rain that pulled the river from its banks.

Months before, your mother waded through water
up to her thighs, wrestled with your brother's bicycle

left out on the front lawn overnight. Even then, you protested
by kicking—tiny feet pounding, not fluttering.

Now, you smell flood waters before the waves swell:
faint sulfur mixed with the moist dirt of a new garden.

You hear the water before it spills, before it rushes
towards West Main, lifting up swings at the park,

tossing toy buckets in backyard sandboxes,
washing through the first floors of homes,

soaking carpets and furniture, leaving dark puddles
and debris in all the cracks and corners.

You know the river is angry, even before the water swirls
around the worn trucks in Old Sam Johnson's backyard,

before it floods Suzy's Bar & Grill, slurping at floorboards
and barstools and torn screens in the doors.

While everyone else listens to the rage after the water rolls
well above flood stage, only you can hear how the river

quietly curses before it crests, its muted voice
Enough, enough, enough, a whisper in the air.

FISHBONES

In late April, the water still too cold for wading,
I clung to the edge of Bill Gardener's Pond,

looking for bones of black crappie and bluegill
caught in brown grass or the winter-slivered cattails.

I discovered the local creeks held more promise:
with the tip of my shoes, I nudged aside stones,

and wrestled fish heads and rotting fins from
the shallow pools where locals gutted their catch.

Once, I caught an old fishing hook in the ball
of my finger, rinsed my hand in the water,

watched the red disappear from my skin.
At home, I lined up my collection on the porch banister,

sure that every ripple spoke through the bones,
that a brook trout would announce

the water was *cold but clear*, the perch
would murmur *shallow* like a hushed sigh.

Muffled whispers of the water drowned out
the way everyone around me laughed.

Later that summer, when thousands of dead carp
floated to the shores of the local reservoir,

their bones sharp, eye sockets empty but staring,
so much that local residents swore they dreamed

of dead fish in their sleep, I wanted to say
You should have been listening.

WARNINGS FOR GIRLS WHO WADE IN TOO MUCH WATER

Be careful. You already know not to wade into rapids,
to watch for undertows, especially in high water.

But every ripple has danger. Near the old mines,
orange rust coats the streams, choking fish and crabgrass.

The cow pasture creeks near the county line are little more
than trickles of water, until a sudden downpour bends grassy banks

turning fields into swamps swarming with black flies and mosquitos.
Even the town river is thick brown, too dark to see

what hides beneath the current: broken beer bottles,
dented cans, corroded car parts, even the occasional fishhook.

Shopping carts and bicycles rest half submerged,
near a rock-punctured *No Dumping* sign.

Take off your socks and shoes. Real girls learn to toughen
the soles of their feet on sharp edges of river stones and fish bones.

During dry spells, you will become desperate, looking for puddles
at the local car wash or parking lots, where water

is often speckled with tar or shining with car oil.
Just watch. If you wade long enough, you will see

permanent stains on your skin, a thin waterline tattooed
above your ankle, or midcalf, or reaching just below your knee.

Accept your fate. This is how all river town girls are—
drawn to water no matter the history or color.

TO THE GIRL WHO BELIEVES ROADKILL WILL RISE
FROM THE DEAD

It's the last days, you are sure. The moon turned red in May,
the earth trembles under the weight of the new interstate.

For the trumpet will sound, and the dead will be raised,
says the new preacher. He shakes with spirit and sweat,

spits out *Corinthians*, when he cites the verse.
You are only six, know death from brittle burnt moths

your mother swipes from the backyard bug zapper, from roadkill
you see along Route 62. Brown bats folded over, their bodies

piled like drop cloths, their wings form pointed stars,
porcupines bristled and splintered against dented guardrails,

opossums in crescent mounds of fur, pink tails trailing
like snapped shoelaces, flattened and smooth.

Your dead will live, the preacher ends his sermon.
You believe him. You have already seen evidence

on the side of the road, blackbird feathers moving
when there is no wind, a raccoon's tail curling

without a breeze. On the way home from church,
you step over a dead robin cradled in gangly ragweed.

Ruffled gray feathers hid a speckled throat and a breast
blotted red. Its beak crushed, its eyes stared ahead,

glassy and surprised. When you go back the next day,
all you will find is a smooth imprint of ironweed

bowing to roadside gravel, green bottle flies, and slivers
of cattails pinning scarlet flecks of down to the ground.

ROADSIDE DEAD

In the thin strips of gravel along Greenbrier Road,
we built kingdoms from roadside debris.

Cigarette butt boats floated in muddy moats,
bent straws propped up wobbling walls

of each pebbled castle. With no one around
to admire our creations, we stood still, pumping

our scrawny arms in the air, listening as truckers
honked their horns, the sound rupturing

the stale summer air that closed in around us.
It was here I first saw death:

A twisted corpse of a deer rested in the clouds
of fine dust. Birds lay splattered, feathers

matted to the road like flies stuck to windshields.
Even the opossum we found nestled near

a speed limit sign taught us lessons
we weren't sure we wanted to learn. Curled

into a comma, its pink tail wrapped around
a limp black foot, its thin pointed face sported

black pebbles for eyes and a mouth that parted
slightly as if struggling for a tight smile.

Sometimes, said my father, *opossums only play dead.*
I was five, so sure of his knowledge that I poked

at the body waiting for a twitch. We only heard
the loud sigh from a semi, as it braked for the sharp curve.

THE FAITH HEALER ON HICKORY STREET

We prayed that day for a classmate
confined to a wheelchair,
for my first-grade teacher
who had suffered another stroke.
I fidgeted, forced to sit through
adult services because my mother
thought I was old enough.
Thick heat bubbled stained glass,
a fly struggled in a web strung
between two worn hymnals.
Shifting, my skirt riding high
with each twitch, my bare calves
brushed against the wooden pew.
I thought of my neighbor
whose gnarled hands once cradled a robin
stunned from a window crash,
how she pressed her thumb to its chest,
pushed twice, three times,
before she paused, waiting to feel more
than the pulse beneath her own skin.

FIRST LESSONS IN LAUNDRY

Our washing machine started spewing
smoke like an old car engine, so my mother
dragged a five-year-old me
to Soaps & Suds on South Main, where
over a month ago, senile Mrs. Dell,
my old Sunday school teacher, said
she saw Jesus in the dryer steam.

That day, quarters rattling in her purse,
my mother taught me to measure soap
without spilling, to turn my father's
pants' pockets inside out and look
for pens or spare change, to dab
white vinegar and water on spots
of mustard and dried mud stains.

Bored, with the laundry finally churning,
and my mother tucked away reading
magazines published six months ago,
I looked for Jesus in the laundry carts
that hobbled on worn-out wheels,
and in t-shirts, torn and listless,
forgotten in dusty table corners.

I imagined the beard, the kind eyes,
the smile, everything I always saw
in Bible story picture books.
But I only heard my mother curse

when she found untreated grass stains
or clumps of powdered soap
that didn't dissolve in the wash.

TOUCHING THE TWO-HEADED CALF

On one of her monthly excursions to buy eggs
from a local farm, my mother stood bargaining
outside the barn, while I wandered inside

to find it standing in its pen, both faces
turning towards me. Rubbing one nose
against the splintered beams, the cow watched me

with four dark eyes, gentle and curious, so I reached
out to touch an ear, the light blue veins
pulsing through skin, thin as my own wrists.

Stretching to the tips of my toes, I balanced
on a bale of hay, and swept my hand over
its forehead, finding a spot of white curly fur,

silky as milkweed seeds broken free.
One mouth chewed slowly, then snorted,
both heads jerking away from my touch.

The whole barn stood still: rafter sparrows
ceased chattering, a gnat stopped struggling
in the spiderweb above me. I held my breath.

Suddenly, its tail snapped at a fly, and its whole body
shuddered, four legs trembling under the weight.
I felt my mother yank me back, a *Don't touch* spoken

with only a sharp pull. There was something here, in the smell of manure, in the creak of barn lofts and rafters, that she was sure would hurt me.

THE FISHING HOLE

The fish aren't biting and I was bored.
Sneakers untied, shoelaces dragging
and dirty, I balanced on the banks,
watching a muddy reflection of a girl

whose ponytail had worked its way loose.
When I slipped into the ripples with a splash,
my father frowned and said, *You will scare
away what fish are left.*

I wandered away to find a fire
pit bored into the bank, wood burnt
black, stones kicked out of place.
Cigarette butts smashed against the ground,

the sun caught the glint of a beer can.
In the shadows, a thin girl leaned
against a striped maple, her skin pale
as the bones of a gutted fish or a paper birch.

A dark-haired boy slid his hands
up her shirt, caressing her rib cage.
His hands were dirty. Fingerprints stained
the soft parts of flesh just above her hips.

Her sighs catapulted insects into the air.
I cupped my hands toward each jump,
and caught a single cricket. Its wings pulsed
in the grimy palms of my hands.

HOW WE LEARNED TO WEAR HEELS

We started early, stole our mothers' wedges, our aunts' stilettos.
Stuffing newspaper in the toes, we made every shoe fit.

Our world a catwalk, we practiced balancing on construction planks,
railroad ties, porch banisters. We sauntered across Laurel Run,

where thick concrete slabs carried us over a trickle of a creek
that cracked dry when summer finally lost its dew. We held

our heads high, as if balancing books for good posture and swayed
our thin hips and thighs. When we clapped, the hills caught.

our applause, tossed the echoes high. We teetered through
our teens, wore heels on first dates, waded through the mud

of Friday night derbies, sawdust kicked up from carnival grounds.
At our high school proms, we dyed our satin shoes to match

our dresses: teal, tangerine, fuchsia—shades perfect until we stepped
in puddles and watched splotches stain our feet, and the bright

colors swirl away in gutters, water gulping without making a sound.

WHY THE RAIN GUTTERS RATTLED

The scratches were not the soft drip
of water after a light spring rain so my father,

sure the culprit was *some kind of stuck critter*,
took his toolbox outside to take apart the gutter.

I had watched chipmunks dive into the plastic pipes,
skittering, clattering all the way to the bottom,

so I imagined one had lost its balance,
turning and twisting itself into a tight somersault,

neck curved forward, head pushed into its chest,
tail curled between its hind legs, paws scrambling.

I had seen dead mice tangled in traps,
flies that had long since stopped struggling

while stuck in spiderwebs, so I wanted something
to break free, the same way I longed to pull my hair

from its braid, or strip away my t-shirt and jeans,
hemlines and seams that cinched my body tight.

I watched my father slip apart the pieces that rattled
under his fingers and a chipmunk tumbled out,

body unraveling in the grass, spine stretching
until its stripes straightened, until its legs

stood steady, until its round eyes stopped blinking
in the light, as if surprised help had come, and how.

ROADKILL GIRLS

We fled summer's heat for the shade
of Sycamore Road. Barefoot and cat scratched,
we posed as princesses, wearing cockleburs
as crowns, blue chicory for corsages.
We sidestepped beer cans, kicked whiskey bottles
filled with thick pools of tobacco spit. Bones
rested in gravel nests near guardrails,
whole skeletons scattered by tractors
and old pickup trucks. We knew what peered
out from behind the purple thistle, what
curled around bent speed limit signs.
For every antler or loose feather, we found
groundhog teeth, a set of claws, soft wisps
of a rabbit's tail. We grew brave, flicked
maggots from fresh kill, the dull thud
of soft bodies hitting tree bark reminding us
of june bugs hurling against back doors
and bedroom windows. At the end of each day,
we whisked our treasures home, decorated
our rooms. The skulls on our dressers
never scared us, even when a jaw curved
into a smile or the empty eye sockets winked.
With every bone, we planned our new world,
starting with a rib we wrestled from a dead raccoon.

II.

SURVIVING THE RUST BELT APOCALYPSE

That summer when the world was ending,
we teetered on railroad tracks, bare feet hardened
against hot metal, and swam late at night
in the gravel pit pond on old Galveston Road.
On dares and double dares, we scaled
chain-link fences and took potshots

at closed factory windows where darkness
scowled through broken glass. We ran
at the first blue flash of a police siren,
tumbling through tall weeds, our escape route
snagged with thistle that snapped under
our feet. We spray painted messages on boxcars

parked in the East End Railroad Yard:
THE END IS NEAR or *HAL LINDSEY WAS HERE*,
and the next morning squirmed through
hot Sunday school sermons, the minister
preaching hellfire and brimstone.
Everything was burning.

Cigarette butts smoldered on the hot pavement,
blue car exhaust lingered in sidewalk cracks
and ripped screen doors. When a string
of fires set to the abandoned businesses
on North Broad Street became the adult talk
of grocery store lines, we knew we had to leave.

We walked to Bill Johnson's farm pasture,
where we fed his horses apples, naming them
for what we knew of the end: *Death, Hunger,*
War, Pestilence—the last word slurring from our lips
as whispers of those nights filled with bourbon and Coke,
how each swallow burned, but we still wanted more.

HOW THE PLAGUES OF EGYPT HIT RURAL PENNSYLVANIA

With our bare thighs sticking to church pews
and our chicken pox scabs scratched into scars,

we squirmed under the weight of golden calves
and commandments, fidgeted in a June

heavy with horse flies. Shortcuts home
were thick woods filled with cicada shells

that cracked under our feet. Creeks rippled
red from the clay mines, gurgled

with bullfrogs. Hailstorms draped
early dusks over dinner, sparked power lines

into blue flickers, drove gnats into streetlights,
car high beams, the screen of our front door.

For days, my father talked of Don Mitchell's cows,
how they were slowly dying in the shade

and no one knew why. With my oldest brother
safely tucked away at summer camp, I watched

Jimmy Evans, the next firstborn I knew, laughing, riding
his bike every morning, his shadow shrinking by noon.

TO THE GIRL WHO BELIEVES THE APOCALYPSE
WILL BEGIN IN A COW PASTURE

You were the only one to see one of the Horsemen
in the hind leg of a Holstein cow, wild hair

and two beady eyes hiding in a black patch
just below a halo smear of mud. You knew

the trickle of the pasture creek would overflow
weeks before the spring melt, that summer

would bring pokeberries mistaken for blackberries,
milkweed pods that split into wisps of red seeds.

You were the first to hear the meadowlark's clear whistle
turn into garbled song. When the hailstorms hit,

you split every ball of ice, released the grasshoppers
trapped inside. You found honeybees caught

inside the clenched fists of Queen Anne's lace.
A prophet in braids and Daisy Duke shorts,

you saw knots in barbed wire fence as knuckles
twisted in prayer. Still, no one listened

when you pulled a thin blade of grass taut
between your thumbs and blew a shrill whistle.

ON BROKEN HOLLOW BRIDGE

Answering Darlene Miller's snotty dare,
I hoisted myself up to the handrail,

thick as a balance beam, but slick
with summer rain and wet rust.

Knees bent, arms out to my sides,
I straightened, chin up, staring ahead.

Kicking off my sandals, I took
my first tentative steps, peeling corrosion

sticking to my skin, the creak of old hinges
swaying in my ears. Slipping, I landed

on one knee, catching myself
before falling. Later, someone told me

kids watching from below all gasped,
and then cheered and clapped.

I should have heard them. But I didn't.
All I heard was rattling and a low rumble

as if these tracks abandoned for years,
were ready, once again, to carry a train.

YELLOWJACKETS

When my father held his Bic lighter
to the nests in back of the garage,
the gray paper pulp sparked

then blackened. Ashes fell,
coating crawling ivy and clover.
A few yellowjackets fled,

one or two swirled, flying
into the sweaty face of my father,
but most too stunned,

their usual side-to-side swag
of a dance, flailing in the smoke.
When one landed on my arm, I stiffened.

His wings settled into a still gauze,
body coiled in yellow bands,
the same shade as buttercups we held

to our skin, cupping sunlight near our chins.
Every step, careful, quivering, as if neither
of us knew who was supposed to sting.

BURYING THE DEAD

By late June, over twenty birds had crashed
into our living room window. Wings twisted,

eyes dull, their bodies strewn in the grass:
goldfinches with yellow feathers bleached pale

by the sun, starlings that had shed their speckled
winter coats to iridescent purple and green,

even a woodpecker's red head glistening in the dew.
Hating the way my brothers tossed the bodies

into the garbage cans, I chose small burial plots
by the birch trees. Using cigar boxes as caskets,

I tucked each bird inside, feathers wrapped in tissue paper,
sealed the homemade coffins shut with tape

plastered over thumbtacks. My brothers all laughed,
and my mother shook her head, wondering

as I struggled with a heavy shovel and hard dirt
that refused to yield to my earnest shoves.

Only my father offered to help, his thick palms folding
over my fingers to push my stick crosses into the ground.

I watched as he placed his heavy boot on the blade,
and the soil cracked and then broke, as he showed me how to dig.

THE WATER TOWER

The summer everyone in town got religion,
two local boys, on a six-drink dare,
scaled the water tower, scrawled
Amanda Forever in neon pink paint.
Everyone admired the curve of the *m*,

the round belly of the *d*, then talked
about the men from M&A Products,
how just off second shift, they spotted
Christ in the closed consignment shop
on the corner of Center Street and South Main.

Not hard to find a god here, said my father,
in a town he claimed was made of churches
and bars. I knew he was right. I counted crosses
and Coors signs, until I ran out of fingers.
I watched for a savior in the chipped plywood

that bound the town stores in a tight fist, saints
in real estate signs buckling under buckshot.
Even my brother's truck went unwashed
and scrutinized, with neighborhood kids
made out bearded faces in the muddy debris.

Seeing nothing but dirt, I turned toward
the water tower, altar of steel and fiberglass,
and looked for Amanda in the tattooed woman
who scooped Rocky Road at the ice cream parlor,
in the girl who pumped gas at the last

full-service station in town, in the young cashier
at Sam's Superette, who stood twirling
strands of hair around her ring finger
and counted change backwards
into the hard palms of construction men.

TIRE TRACKS

Just north of town, the Johnson boys wore
fields raw with their three wheelers,
while my Uncle Paul parked his truck

in our garage and then disappeared
with a woman who wasn't my Aunt Fran.
Too young for a real job at Pete's Pizzeria

I watched the Barker twins for less than $3 an hour,
their Big Wheels flying down our front sidewalks
in a rattle of hard plastic and uneven pavement.

For weeks, thick black smoke clouded our streets.
Everyone muttered, *The tire heap at R&J's Junkyard*,
but no one said the words out loud, just like no one

talked about the Caldwell girls who died
in the two-vehicle collision near Cable Run Road
or how the other driver, beer bottles clicking

in his back seat, walked away, with only a bruise
on his cheek. To get away from the burning rubber,
I bummed a ride to Miller's Pond, wearing

my big sister's swimming suit that sagged
in all the wrong places. Swinging on an old tire
strung high above the stagnant water, hot treads

burned my bare thighs, while miles away,
police measured the skid marks left at the crash site,
ignoring the chipped metallic paint and broken glass.

FLYPAPER

During the hottest part of that summer,
black flies flooded our kitchen,
buzzing through window blinds
and near light bulbs, refusing to die.
They dodged the long curls of flypaper

hoisted near the sink and garbage cans,
only occasionally getting caught.
I watched as some jerked
in a spastic dance and then tore free,
leaving bits of their legs and wings behind.

With flyswatters, my brothers
took turns smashing, trapping bodies
on stove burners and countertops,
counting the number of hits it took
before the shuddering flies

would finally lie still. In between
every sharp slap, we listened
as our parents fought about money
and the heat, their words convulsing
through the stagnant air, until

I covered my ears so I couldn't hear.
At night, when I fell asleep, my dreams
filled with butterflies caught in backyard grills,
blackbirds and blue jays diving
into bedroom windows, an opossum,

head tangled in barbed wire, twisting
until the metal folded in, clutching its throat.
Wings and feathers, tufts of fur, a long,
hairless pink tail—when I woke, what
I remembered most was the twitching.

MAYFLIES

When the mayflies finally hatched that year,
my bedtime ghost stories came alive.

Thousands of wings rose in hazy halos above
Millstone Run, covering the little league field,

concealing the outfield, pitcher's mound,
home plate. My brother's game called

because no one could make out the pop flies
or foul lines, we drove home, my father

edging the car slowly through thin flutters
that turned the late afternoon to a milky dusk.

The next day we woke to reminders that at times,
we lived among the dead. My mother swept bodies

from the front porch and raked our yard
free from insect debris. Still, I found wings

in cracks of the sidewalk, in the screen door,
even in cobwebs strung between porch railings.

MY SUMMER AS SIPHONED GAS

Lines of Ford trucks and station wagons
wrapped gas stations in folded layers
of exhaust. Hot tar speckled afternoons,
side streets greased with trickles of oil
puckered under the weight of potholes.

Dressed in a terry cloth romper and dirty
sneakers that would never stay tied,
I watched my brother park his old pickup
in the front yard, prop open the hood
with a thick plank of wood. He hunched

over, t-shirt full of holes and grease spots,
his hands juggling screwdrivers and spare
parts. A lit cigarette dangled from the corner
of his mouth, close to the sputtering engine.
Some days I offered to help, hand him

loose parts, adjust the radio to his favorite
station so that the static stopped crinkling
the heat, but most days, I followed
the neighbor boy to the old cars tucked
in the tall weeds behind Tom's Towing and Parts.

Only ten, he already knew how to hot-wire
his father's Jeep, how to build a bicycle
from two wheels and an old handlebar.
His mission that summer: to find
every bit of fuel left in our small town.

He pried open gas caps, slipped in a garden hose,
sucked until he drew a few drops
of gas. Turning away my offer to help,
he picked up my chin, looked at my sunburned lips.
Even a small cut, he said, *will sting.*

SPLINTERED

The local lumber mill gave us singed mornings
where we played hide-and-seek in the soft haze.
We climbed the branches of crab apple trees,
peered from behind log piles our fathers kept high
for a winter we couldn't imagine in the heat.
The best place was under the back porch,
where I could listen to the paperboy pulling

his red wagon, kid sister and newsprint in tow,
wheels a scratchy echo of faraway thunder
and a yellow sky that refused to crack open.
I watched other kids run screaming
Olly olly oxen free, and my mother snap the clothesline,
where a layer of dust lingered on her laundry days,
the cloud a wisp of unwished dandelion seeds.

I stayed hidden until after lunchtime was called,
listening to the grown-up talk creak above me.
A house on River Run Road had collapsed into a pile
of wooden slivers and termites. For months,
my father explained, the neighbors said
they heard *chewing*. Every day moved a bit slower.

Dusks wilted a little more, nights burned,
while the moon shrunk to a thin chip of wood in the sky.
I watched a branch holding my tire swing break,
a teeter-totter split into two. Unvarnished porch railings

beckoned me, even when a sliding shortcut
to home base snagged my jeans, split the soft skin
of my thighs into thin beads of blood.

SECONDHAND HARMONICA

I saw it at one of my mother's yard sale excursions.
Crusted with rust, the handle wore a dent
the same size as a small thumbprint.
Cool metal in my hands, I blew through the reeds,
the hollow sound reminding me of wind
right before a late summer thunderstorm,

but when I inhaled, I heard the grind
of AC/DC and Def Leppard, hard rhythms
that rocked our garage for weeks.
My brother's new hangout hosted friends
with long hair and ripped shirts and girls
wearing cutoff jeans and tank tops,
their bodies curved like swirls of cigarette smoke.

Stop, my mother said, when she heard me,
yanking the instrument from my lips.
You don't know where that's been.
But I did know. I could taste my new braces.
I could taste smoke and peppermint gum
and cherry lip gloss. I could taste spit.

SKINNY-DIPPING WITH ST. ANTHONY

In those early August days, your mother prayed
for everything she could not find: car keys,
a matching sock, one pearl earring, your father's lost job.
When she wasn't looking, you too disappeared,

mostly at dusk, when it was easy to get lost
lured by our favorite swimming hole,
where we stripped to our t-shirt tan lines.
I was still mostly boy: chest flat, thin buds

of breasts little more than pinched skin.
Late bloomer, my mother once said,
although I didn't know yet what was going to blossom.
You were a scrawny stick with sharp collarbones

and skinny shoulders, a medal of a dead saint
resting on a rope around your neck.
We pushed through cattails and thin cobwebs
that formed in evening dew, flicked away

water bugs that seemed to skate above the waves.
Even when our teeth chattered in the cool air
and our skin puckered from the pinch
of the water, you never wanted to venture

towards home. You knew what you would find:
your mother, standing on the back porch praying
to St. Anthony, calling for him so loudly
we both thought for sure God had a new name.

WHY I STOPPED CATCHING BEES

Old coffee cans smothered every buzz
in a stale whiff of morning brew, so I chose
canning jars as my weapons, snapping
glass around bee and blossom, mastering
a sharp click without any cracks.
I wanted their haughty hues,
their proud hum, so at night I lined
my windowsill with jars,
each punctured lid squeezed tight.
The start of school brought Cindy Mills,
the first in fifth grade to wear a bra.
Once a thin twirl of a girl who danced
on the playground in circles, she showed
me the year before how to spin
without feeling dizzy. I watched her
in English class that day, saw her shrink
into a shadow. Slouched forward,
shoulders hunched, her whole body curved.
When the boys pointed to her chest, yelled
beestings, she only sunk lower,
her scowl melting parts of the front row.
I ran home under the swell of her thick glare,
stared at my collection, at the limp bodies
banded in bright colors, stranded soft in pyres
of dead flowers and grass, before I threw open
my screenless window to toss them high
into the air, hoping one more time
to see a quick shimmy, a lofty shake.

TO THE GIRL WHO TALKED TO SUMMER INSECTS

It all began when your father started staying out too late.
You waited by the front door, palms pressed against

a ripped screen checkered with gnats and mosquitos.
When a speckled moth landed, flexed its wings

beneath your fingers, you whispered the dangers
of a snagged wire or a careless brush of a hand.

You were surprised when it listened, then flew away.
When you heard june bugs pound the bedroom windows,

you admired their courage, but told them it was no use.
You are never getting inside. You cupped ladybugs

in your hands for luck, apologized to the glint
of the green and gold beetles you flicked away,

desperate to save your mother's tomato plants.
Some insects were silent, others angry or lost:

a paper wasp fumed when your brother knocked its nest
from the garage roof, a single cricket sawed its wings, chirped.

Even now, when you are old enough to know better,
you walk by a vacant lot where a single katydid calls for winter.

Its mantra, *Kate, Kate, Kate* is so insistent,
you have come to believe that is your name.

THE SUMMER OF MAN-MADE MIRACLES

I dumped grape juice into Gallagher Run,
hoping the muddy swirls would turn into wine,
and pretended the stale angel food cake
old Mrs. Rogers threw to the birds was really
manna from heaven. Evenings, I decided,

were the best times for miracles, as I plucked
moths from back porch lights and swept
them into the air, hoping a few singed wings
would flutter in the thin twilight strands.
In the kitchen, my mother canned tomatoes,

sauce splattering, hot steam plastering
gray strands of hair to her forehead.
She talked on the phone as if speaking to God.
Everything needed divine intervention.
My brother's truck that gargled and rattled,

would need a miracle to get through the summer.
My sister, who stayed out long past curfew
and wore shorts that cupped her thighs tight
would need a miracle to get through high school.
And my father, who paced the floor, cigarette

in his mouth, a lighter in his hand, *would need
a miracle to get a job at his age.* I listened,
scraping a black beetle from a spider's web,
placing it on the picnic table. Even free, its wings
twitched, its body shuddered, but refused to fly.

TO THE GIRL WHO WANTED TO BE A
ROADSIDE WEED

Even at eight, you knew you were going to leave.
Thistle nipped, blackberry bush scratched,

you twitched your skinny pinched hips
and fled town without shoes, soles hardened

by beestings and the toothed leaves of dandelions.
With your hair tangled like an old bird's nest,

your lips cracked and burned by the sun,
you wore cutoff jean shorts and an orange tank top

the same shade as spotted jewelweed or a tiger lily.
With every blistered scab, you became the red bloom

of Queen Anne's lace, your budding bruises
by your bare ankles turned you into purple asters.

When a car pulled over and a family spilled out,
you felt for sure this was your escape:

a child picked you as part of a dandelion bouquet,
stem bleeding milk as you nestled in her sticky hands.

A teenage girl thought you were a daisy and plucked you apart:
He loves me, he loves me not—smiling at the last petal.

III.

WAYS OF WRITING RUST

Use a red pen. Push a full moon through every line.
Scribble down an old barn and a children's game of tag

that ends with a nail's scratch and tetanus shot.
Remember to cross all your Ts. Save

the graffiti, the sharp letters and language,
even if you are not sure if the words are a Bible verse

or lyrics from an old rock and roll song.
Scrawl down corner bars and closed stores.

Pluck the jewels from Queen Anne's lace, throw away
the white blossoms, but keep the sunflowers and tiger lilies.

Never use a pencil. You won't want to erase.
But always proofread. Just cross out the spring trillium,

the first frost, bedsheets that bounce in the breeze.
Use every margin. Stencil the last railroad trestles,

roadside mailboxes sealing shut with orange crust,
a bicycle left out overnight, its spokes turning.

Trace the Z shape of fire escapes and the half hearts
of coke ovens. Scribe the sighs of girls who want boys

drunk with dares and drivers' licenses, boys who drive
through traffic lights and railroad crossings, flashing.

And mothers who teach their daughters to cut away,
but slice apples with knife blades coming towards them.

BRAMBLES

Sitting on the worn path, I sucked
a wounded thumb, watching
my mother wade through thickets
of long, thorny stems. She claimed
the best berries, black as shiny tar

and plump with wild juice, were always
near the top. Thorns pulled her hair,
grabbed at her shirt, but she wore
each prick with a tight smile.
Nearby, catbirds feasted, a chipmunk,

cheeks quivering, scrambled to hide
in the brush. I studied the rotting logs
covered with moss, beer cans
and cigarette butts left over
from a local teen party, then pushed

my finger to my thumb as a single bead
of blood sprang from the spot
where I had reached for ripeness.
Years later, my first boyfriend, wild
with beer, drove his dirt bike through

this same brush while I sat behind him,
clutching his waist, my fingers hooked
around the belt loops of his jeans.

Boots protected my feet, jeans covered my thighs, yet at home, I still found scratches where thorns found my skin.

WHERE GIRLS STILL RIDE THE BEDS OF PICKUP TRUCKS

The wind is always is warm here. Breezes snap
through their t-shirts, hot metal and sun burn

their arms and bare legs. They stand
near the cabs, kneel by the rattling tailgates.

It's here where they learn how to catch maple seeds
in their teeth, and how to spit them out.

Here, they learn how to dig pebbles
and bits of gravel from beneath their skin.

Some say their bodies turned hollow,
one could hear wind whistling through their collarbones

and shoulder blades. Some say they almost sprout wings.
But they never fly. They only learn how to balance.

Even now, you will know them, these girls
who survived quick trips to grocery stores,

wrong turns on narrow one-way streets,
even moving days, when they sat propped up,

steadying chipped coffee tables and couches.
Their ponytails are tangled with knots

that never unraveled from the way the wind
always combed through their long hair.

RENAMING THE CONSTELLATIONS

When your father finally left for good,
we stole Jim Beam from his secret stash,
and staggered to your splintered tree house,

where we once played tea parties
with our teddy bears, and where now, we teetered
on floorboards rotting with moss and mildew.

We pushed aside leaves and branches, pointing
to what we thought we knew about the sky. Here,
the Little Dipper was a mug with a long handle,

and the Big Dipper, a saucepan, the same kind
your mother used for Chef Boyardee
when she was too hot and too tired to cook.

With my brother's telescope, we outlined
clusters of stars splattered across the sky,
the ones that could look like real diamonds,

but we knew we were more like rhinestones,
cheap gems sparkling like Kmart jewelry
that lay scattered across our big sisters' dressers.

CROW SEASON

When a car backfires in the alley behind me,
I remember those summer afternoons that broke
under the weight of BB shots, and how I hid
in my bedroom, so I couldn't hear
my brothers turning telephone lines
into target practice, birds into twisted tailspins.

From their kill, they propped bodies against
our backyard woodpile, dark wings splayed
like black paper fans. The best feathers
were plucked for the junior high girls
who twirled shafts of soft down through
barrettes and friendship bracelets.

They circled the playground, a murder
of girls wrapping fingers around loose
strands of hair, their bras' thin silhouettes
beneath crisp cotton t-shirts, sharp hip bones
jutting against jean waistbands. The leader,
a sheer shadow of a young woman,

chewed gum, blew bubbles just to pucker her lips.
Knotting stiff feathers in my hair, I colored
my skin with my sister's mascara, caught
the hard *caw!* in back of my throat.
Then I spun in the August heat until I could fly,
until I could show every last crow what to do.

THE LORE OF L&J'S JUNKYARD

Tanned with summer sun and dirt,
the neighborhood boys braved the jungle,
hacked their way through thick thistle
and foxtail with bats splintered
from last year's losing little league season.
They kicked aside exhaust pipes,
stomped on old license plates,
tore a truck door from the last creak
of its hinges. Their stories swarmed

with car hoods crinkled like paper fans,
mufflers streaked with road salt saliva,
windows splattered into spiderwebs
of chipped glass. Only feral cats survived,
basking on the hoods of sunbaked Studebakers.
Scrawny with patchwork fur and tails
the shape of stickpins, they chewed
on car cushions, and drank antifreeze
until green drops seeped from their whiskers.

For weeks, I watched as they pulled parts
from the wreckage, two mud flaps, a rearview mirror,
a cracked carburetor. Their clubhouse
became a garage lit by dim flashlights
and a single candle. When I saw the shadow
of a steering wheel, I knew they were serious.
Word was they were building a getaway car.
At night, oil leaked onto my pillow, hammers pounded

in my sleep. Even now, with every back road,
I still see their attempts at flight: tire tread,
broken mufflers, hubcaps twisted with rust.

STILL LIFE WITH BEST FRIEND AND SCARECROW

The last year of your family's farm,
we took credit for the crops,
told everyone it was the scarecrow
we had built months before. He stood
stiff and stuffed, splinters for bones,
straw as skin scratching stonewashed jeans
and a red football jersey blotched pink
by the bright sun. Autumn brought corn,
husks green, ears heavy, rows bowing
low to the ground. We shook kernels
from the folds of our t-shirts, found tassels
tangled in our hair, silk snagged in the soles
of our boots. Weeks before, Joe Miller
asked you out, and you turned him down, twice.
For nights, he parked at the end of the road.

We only saw the shadow of his Ford,
his silhouette in the driver's seat,
but we imagined his forehead furrowed,
like a burlap bag pinched by a hard frost,
his smirk pulled tight above chin stubble,
clipped short and uneven, a field
after the last harvest. A thin strand
of cigarette smoke twirled around
his left thumb. But we weren't afraid.
We were country girls who carried penknives
in our pockets, kept our fingernails
long. *Stalking*, we would call it now.

But back then, we wouldn't
have known that word. We would
have thought it had something
to do with the corn.

MILKWEED PODS

I slept with a souvenir seashell next to my ear.
      It was September, I wasn't yet seven. Still warm enough
to prop my bedroom window open, I listened

for the footsteps of my father on the front porch,
      his out-of-work stance a shadow lit only
by a cigarette. I didn't understand why my mother

flipped through Sunday papers for coupons,
      why she stopped putting money for next year's vacation
in the wine jug that sat near the cellar stairs.

When I packed my summer clothes away,
      I shook stray grains of sand from my sandals,
wondered if I could smell saltwater forever.

I looked for answers in the fields behind my house,
      where I brushed aside cockleburs, pushed away
sharp leaves of sow thistles that poked at the air.

Near the trail, I picked prickly pods, scraped
      away clingy crab spiders. Sap lingered
on the palms of my hands. With my thumb, I split

the seams, pressed ripped plants to my ears.
      I could hear the chortle of the town's river, the drone
of factories in a metallic round of cricket song.

SANCTUARY

The September before I turned seven,
I fell in love with the old church
on Benton Run Road. Straight-backed and stiff,
its doors padlocked like the closed factories
on South Main, the building guarded
a graveyard garnished with goldenrod,

and wild geranium, herded marble lambs
white as ghost birch trees. Secluded
but never silent, a stray breeze rocked
the steeple's bell, caught webs strung
between tombstones, shook spiders
and stray petals from faded bouquets.

When my father's swing shifts brought
the late summer heat into our home,
I fled through broken windows, crawled
through split glass without a cut.
Inside, the pulpit lay splintered,
a firepit gutted knotted floorboards.

Footprints black with ashes trailed
across pews. Fingerprints smeared across
smudged glass. I thumbed through torn Bibles,
Old Testaments torn from the New,
and hymnals ripped into black specks of notes.
Here, God smelled liked burned paper.

THE GIRL WHO PARTED MILL CREEK WITH HER TOES

At that last Sunday School picnic, I tossed
my sandals to the shore and waded through

the shallow water, trying to ignore the grown-up talk
of factory closings, lost jobs, and foreclosures.

Mass exodus, the minister's wife joked about our town
as she tossed the salad. My mother responded

by calling to me, *Don't go where I can't see you.*
In the clatter of plastic forks, someone asked about my father.

I knew the word, *Exodus,* from the way Becky Reynolds
almost choked on the *x* when she was showing off

by reciting the books of the Bible. I knew about Moses,
the gray beard and Ten Commandments.

He reminded me of my father who hadn't shaved in days
and sat at home, daily newspaper in hand,

reading want ads and obituaries,
but mostly doing nothing, hands folded in front of him.

Across the stream, the Miller boys lifted rocks
and laughed as crawfish darted away from them,

Sara Thompson picked a dandelion for her hair,
and Becky stumbled through *Obadiah* and *Joel*.

I flexed my toes in the water and the waves parted
around my ankles. A few feet away from me,

Jimmy Wilson's little sister dropped her cherry Popsicle
in the current. I watched as the ripples turned red.

COLD SNAP

Days after Bill Johnson's youngest boy
    drove his truck through his family farm's chicken coop,
I plucked feathers from the air, picked red maple leaves
    to press between pieces of wax paper, discovered
condom wrappers caught in the thorns
    of our rose garden. *Boys*, my mother muttered,

picking latex from leaves, pausing only to watch me,
    a hard line creasing the band of skin between her eyes.
That October I was ten, already knew what most
    farm girls knew, that chickens without heads
didn't dance, but twitched, that a sharp axe
    made a clean cut with little blood. Still, I jumped

when a stick snapped, when my brothers cracked
    the skulls of trout they brought home for dinner.
From the attic window, I watched the bonfires
    the Johnsons held every Saturday, listened
for the sharp pop and spray that sprang
    from beer cans, held my breath when Joey,

the second-to-oldest, grabbed a girl by a belt loop,
    pulled her close. I knew who she was. She sold
corn at her father's stand in town, wore her red hair
    in two braids, her jeans cuffed instead of hemmed.
In the shadows he was all flannel and fingers. He bent
    her neck back so far I thought she would break.

CAUGHT EATING APPLES

I've been here before. Usually, at dusk, when the sky
wears thin, when gray bark and broad leaves fade

into dull shadows, when my sneakers, soaked
with dew, slide as I start to climb. I have learned

how to balance on branches, how to hoist
myself up, feet lodged against tree knots and burs.

The best apples are always near the top.
I know to avoid bruised skin, dark holes where

worms have burrowed in. I even know how to spit
seeds, lips puckering as if whistling or waiting

for a kiss. I've been taught how to twist each stem,
reciting the alphabet with each turn.

When the stem snaps free, I'm told I will marry
a boy whose name begins with that letter.

For weeks, it has been me, the fruit,
and the occasional wild turkey or white-tailed deer

that trail in through the field to feast on the cores.
When I am finally caught and questioned, I don't deny

what I have eaten. I don't say I am hungry.
I only explain I ate because I could.

TO ALL THE GIRLS WHO HAVE SHOPLIFTED LIPSTICK

Maybe you are 17, broke and tired, tips from working at Tami's Café
stored away for car insurance or future college textbooks. There's little

left for makeup or new clothes, and you love the shades that promise
to last through hundreds of *sips, bites, and kisses* but really only stain

bummed cigarettes you smoke on your breaks. Or maybe you are 14,
and on a dare you slip *Plum* or *Pretty Peach* into your purse, listening

to the gasp of your giggly friends. Or maybe you are 10, wearing
your sister's clothes, hemlines dragging, a waistline that dips and sags

from your nonexistent hips. Already, you reason, you are forced
to be like her, resentment hanging like her old jean jacket off

your skinny shoulders, the contraband Cover Girl colors held tightly
in your fist. Or maybe you are only 6, slipping a fat ChapStick tube

into your mother's purse even after she told you *No*. You think
it will taste like pink lemonade. You like the pale pink, the way

it looks like the soft pads on your cat's feet or pieces of chewed
bubble gum someone has spit out onto the street.

WHY THERE ARE STILL GIRLS WHO WASH THEIR HAIR IN BEER

Foam spills like suds through their fingers.
Streams of water splash, massage their scalps,

trickle down the napes of their necks. Yellow pools
settle in the shallow hollows of their collarbones.

Beads stick to their shoulders, to the skin
above their breasts. One girl says Straub

makes her hair shiny, while another explains
that with a mixture of Heineken and hairspray,

her hair will finally hold a curl. Another swears
she uses Michelob because the man she's been seeing

for six months now, kisses her right temple,
says she could be happy hour at Suzy's Bar & Grill.

Sometimes, when she's upset, she chews a strand like she did
when she was a child. She wants to taste what he tastes.

ALL MY BOYFRIENDS WORE BEER LABELS
FOR NICKNAMES

At 15, Rocky rolled with every punch.
He could jump start a truck with a spray

of Pepsi and a frayed extension cord, hot-wire
a car with a bent paper clip or thin hairpin.

His jaw was a bent tailgate, his eyes gray
as aluminum siding. All beard stubble

and grease from his father's garage,
he left oil and Old Spice on my skin,

black fingerprints on my rib cage.
Sam gave up his childhood of Sammy

for grass-stained jeans and a farmer's tan
he wore well into late December.

He wished for red mornings, said the rings
of the moon ran through his veins. Once,

I pulled corn silk from a scratch on his arm, plucked
a beetle burrowing in a blister by his left thumb.

And Bud was for Pal or Friend. Built
like a pool stick, he carried a Bic but didn't smoke,

quit high school but quoted Coleridge, scrawled
fancy script on the rocks by the swimming hole.

Every word left me wondering about the fate
of that albatross. Years later, his truck would whirl

counterclockwise, collide with a waitress
on her way home from work. Some said

he stole her strawberry lip gloss at the scene
of the accident, kept her name tag for a souvenir.

But back when we were both 17, he tasted
like the others, all froth and foam, sour and cold.

STARGAZING UNDER THE INFLUENCE

That night, the bed of your truck was a dance floor,
your grandparents' farm our own private club.
I moved to the rhythm of a bass guitar
and a battery slowly dying. Music moaned
from the radio, old shocks rocked under my feet.
You watched as flecks of rust flew from my heels,

strangely silent with every new scuff mark.
We had the splinter of a Wolf Moon, a single star
shivering, the strange halo of the farmhouse
splintered in the wooden fence shadows.
As I twirled, your gun rack rattled,
drops of beer sprayed. I toasted every flake

of new snow. In the distance, branches reached
out for us, more stick figures than trees, the shadow
of a silo struck a regal pose, ivy sticking out
like loose strands of hair in a girl's tight braid.
Dizzy, I fell to the tailgate, stripped off my coat, stared
at Orion's Belt quivering in the black brow of the sky.

Sweat froze to my temples, cold metal burned
through my thighs. I told you I was sorry
for the night before, how I pushed
you away. *It's not you*, I wanted to say.
I just hated the cold plastic seats of your truck,
how my chapped lips, winter dry, had started to bleed.

LANDSCAPE WITH STARVING DEER

At dusk, their shadows staggered through
two feet of snow towards the orchard,
where they pawed the ground for the last

of the apple cores. They gnawed on trees,
chewed the back porch banisters,
their thin skin stretched around sharp ribs

and hip bones. One night, they raided
our carefully crafted Nativity scene,
the manger turned over, straw gone,

a chipped ceramic Jesus tossed to the side.
I was with my brother when he hit the doe
with his truck, listened as he cursed

when he didn't have his shotgun.
I had long learned the mercy of killing.
The deer stumbled to its feet, stared

at me, eyes milky, breath so thin,
there was no cloud in the cold air.
Later, I picked tufts of hair

from the front grill, listened to my brother
talk to my father. *It wasn't an accident*,
he tried to explain. *More like a suicide.*

THAW

Weeks before any warm weather, I stamped on ice patches
and kicked at crusty snow lodged in every hard-to-reach place:

our family car's tires, the front porch railings, even the soles
of my father's steel-toed boots left on the back steps overnight.

I flung snowballs at icicles that dangled from the roof,
and listened to their dull clatter when they hit the ground.

Plastic gutters drooped and bent under the weight of the cold.
Every breath I took was white, every shiver, a tremor.

Still, going inside was no warmer. With a furnace
that spewed high heating bills with little heat, and a strike

looming at my father's factory, I expected to see pale fog
from my parents when they spoke, in trembled tones,

just slight of any kind of anger. It was better outside,
where I wandered to Benson Pond. Frozen over,

the winter-dry weeds, brittle and still, didn't even rustle.
Digging through the snow, I found a flat rock that fit

into the palm of my hand. When I threw it, I knew
in spite of its lift and spin through the air,

it wouldn't skip over the pond's cold surface.
I just wanted something, anything, to crack.

ADVICE FOR ALL THE RUST BELT CASSANDRAS

Let everyone call you Cassie. Or Cass.
Or even Cassie Jo, although you have no middle name.

In the mornings, shake sawdust from your hair,
write your name on both of your wrists,

use a peeling sunburn as blush, braid your hair
with the curls of truck exhaust.

At the nearest corner store, smile at the cashier
who hands back your change, her ten-minute break

lingering on the last dollar bill. Forget
you've known her since grade school, one

of those girls who coughed years before her Camels,
whose skin turned yellow long before

she grew nicotine stains on her fingers.
Don't talk about how lumber mill smoke hovers

too close to every curb, how the saltbox-shaped houses
on South Main snuggle too close to the river.

Don't mention your nightmares of ivy
fingering old farmhouses and factories,

or how the last silo on South Laurel Road will take
a deep breath, forget to exhale, collapse,

drowning a farmer in his own harvest.
Use every dusk. Follow the fireflies.

Walk to the football field, sit under the bleachers,
and watch how sunlight splinters wood, tosses shadows

to cigarette butts and broken beer bottles.
Run your fingers over hearts and initials

that will never be carved. Pray you will walk home
with only mosquito bites and a handful of slivers.

ACKNOWLEDGMENTS

Many thanks to the editors of the journals where these poems (sometimes, in earlier versions with slightly different titles) were first published:

Arsenic Lobster: "The Fishing Hole", "To the Girl Who Talked to Summer Insects"

Autumn Sky Poetry Daily: "Fishbones"

The Barn Owl Review: "How the Plagues of Egypt Hit Rural Pennsylvania"

Blast Furnace: "Advice for All the Rust Belt Cassandras", "The Lore of L&J's Junkyard"

The Bridge Literary Arts Journal: "To All the Girls Who Have Shoplifted Lipstick"

Cæsura: "To the Girl Who Believes the Apocalypse Will Begin in a Cow Pasture"

Cave Wall: "Still Life with Best Friend and Scarecrow"

Chautauqua: "Burying the Dead", "Mayflies", "Why the Rain Gutters Rattled"

Comstock Review: "Flypaper", "Landscape with Starving Deer"

Conte: "My Summer as Siphoned Gas"

Cumberland River Review: "To the Girl Who Can Hear the River Talk"

District Lit: "Caught Eating Apples", "Warnings for Girls Who Wade in Too Much Water"

Escape Into Life: "Auditioning for the Apocalypse", "Cold Snap", "Milkweed Pods," "Thaw"

The Fiddleback: "Roadkill Girls"

Flycatcher: "The Faith Healer on Hickory Street"

Glass: A Journal of Poetry: "Why I Stopped Catching Bees"

Harpur Palate: "Ways of Writing Rust", "Why There Are Still Girls Who Wash Their Hair in Beer", "Skinny-Dipping with St. Anthony"

Masque & Spectacle: "First Lessons in Laundry"

Mud Season Review: "Muskrat Pond", "Roadside Dead". "The Summer of Man-Made Miracles", "Touching the Two-Headed Calf"

The Naugatuck River Review: "Sanctuary", "Splintered"

New Plains Review: "Brambles", "Tire Tracks"

Novus Literary Arts Journal: "The (Almost) Lost Legend of the Lawson Boys"

Paper Street: "The Spring of Hand-Me-Downs"

Pittsburgh Quarterly: "On Broken Hollow Bridge"

Poemeleon: "Surviving the Rust Belt Apocalypse"

Poetry East: "Yellowjackets"

Rattle: "Where the Girls Still Ride the Beds of Pickup Trucks"

River Styx: "All My Boyfriends Wore Beer Labels for Nicknames".

Rust + Moth: "Renaming the Constellations"

Slipstream; "Second-Hand Harmonica"

Spillway: "To the Girl Who Believes Roadkill Will Rise from the Dead"

Sugar House Review: "Crow Season"

SWWIM: "ChapStick"

Tahoma Literary Review: "Tips for Young Girls Hoping to Avoid the Rapture"

The Tusculum Review: "Stargazing Under the Influence"

Whiskey Island: "The Girl Who Parted Mill Creek with Her Toes", "To the Girl Who Wanted to be a Roadside Weed"

"Why I Stopped Catching Bees", formerly titled "The Summer I Stopped Catching Bees" was also featured in the 2011 edition of *The Best of the Net*.

"Yellowjackets" also appeared in Ted Kooser's *American Life in Poetry*.

"Flypaper" won third place in the *Comstock Review*'s Annual Muriel Craft Bailey Memorial Poetry Contest

"Where Girls Still Ride the Beds of Pickup Trucks" will appear in *Keystone: Contemporary Poets on Pennsylvania* (Pennsylvania State University Press, 2025)

Several of these poems also appeared in the chapbooks, *Stealing Dust* (Finishing Line Press, 2009) and *Wearing Heels in the Rust Belt*, winner of Main Street Rag's 2011 Chapbook contest.

THANKS

First and foremost, a big thank you goes to Courtney LeBlanc for giving this book a chance in the world. Another big thank you goes to Jodie Beabout for the photo shoots and the beautiful cover photo. And of course, I can't forget Addalyn who was a wonderful model.

For their careful reading and guidance with these poems, I am grateful to Maggie Anderson, Todd Davis, Jim Daniels, Jeannine Hall Gailey, Neil Shepard, Philip Terman, and Gabriel Welsch who read many versions of these works.

A special thank you goes to Kathleen Kirk, poetry editor of *Escape Into Life*, who always found homes for my poems.

Love and thanks to Sandee Gertz, my Rust Belt sister, for her support of my poems.

To poets Marjorie Maddox, Judith Vollmer, Tony Vallone, and Jerry Wemple, thank you for reminding me how important my home state of Pennsylvania is to my poems.

To my mentor and advisor Diane Payne, thank you for your support of my work (even though you know me more as a creative nonfiction writer than a poet!)

Sending gratitude to Sarah Rossey, Jessica Weible, and the rest of the crew at Watershed for giving voices to those who live and write in the wilds of Pennsylvania.

Additional gratitude goes to Christina Fisanick and Damian Dressick for helping others hear the voices of Northern Appalachia.

Gratitude goes to my colleagues and students at Jamestown Community College for their support of my work. Thanks also goes to the Writers' Center at the Chautauqua Institution where many of my poems were born.

As always, love and gratitude goes to my family for their love and support of my work.

Finally, my love goes to Anthony for his support of a life that he doesn't always understand, but is willing to try, because he knows how important the writing world is to me.

ABOUT THE AUTHOR

Karen J. Weyant is an Associate Professor of English at Jamestown Community College in Jamestown, New York. Her poems have appeared in a number of journals including *Chautauqua*, *Copper Nickel*, *Crab Orchard Review*, *Harpur Palate*, *Lake Effect*, *Rattle*, *River Styx*, *Spillway*, *Slipstream*, and *Whiskey Island*. She is author of two poetry chapbooks, *Stealing Dusk* and *Wearing Heels in the Rust Belt*; *Avoiding the Rapture* is her first full-length collection. She lives in Warren, Pennsylvania, with her partner, Anthony Patalano, and four unruly felines.

ABOUT THE PRESS

Riot in Your Throat is an independent press
that publishes fierce, feminist poetry.

Support independent authors, artists, and presses.

Visit us online:
www.riotinyourthroat.com

Printed in the USA
CPSIA information can be obtained
at www.ICGtesting.com
LVHW040805060923
757193LV00006B/136